I0814279

WEIRD WORLD

WEIRD STRUCTURES

BY YVETTE LaPIERRE

Core Library

An Imprint of Abdo Publishing
abdobooks.com

Cover image: Casa Batlló in Barcelona, Spain, is famous for the fluid details on its outside face.

abdobooks.com

Published by Abdo Publishing, a division of ABDO, PO Box 398166, Minneapolis, Minnesota 55439.

Printed in the United States of America, North Mankato, Minnesota.
102025
012026

Cover Photo: Luciano Mortula-LGM/Shutterstock Images
Interior Photos: Rudy Mareel/Shutterstock Images, 4–5; Nick Ut/AP Images, 6; Shutterstock Images, 10, 17, 23, 26, 28, 43; Patryk Kosmider/Shutterstock Images, 12–13; Rosemarie Mosteller/Shutterstock Images, 15; Steve Heap/Shutterstock Images, 18; Alan Tan Photography/Shutterstock Images, 20–21, 45; Airbnb/Mega/IBLIM/Newscom, 24; Boaz Rottem/Alamy, 28–29; Dmytro Kolin/Shutterstock Images, 31; Aleksandr Shilov/Shutterstock Images, 32; Jon Bilous/Shutterstock Images, 34–35; Halit Sadik/Shutterstock Images, 37; Exotica/Alamy, 38; Andrei Minsk/Shutterstock Images, 40

Editor: Riley Madsen
Series Designer: Marley Richmond

Library of Congress Control Number: 2025939238

Publisher's Cataloging-in-Publication Data

Names: LaPierre, Yvette, author.
Title: Weird structures / by Yvette LaPierre
Description: Minneapolis, Minnesota: Abdo Publishing, 2026 | Series: Weird world | Includes online resources and index.
Identifiers: ISBN 9781098298517 (lib. bdg.) | ISBN 9798384932314 (ebook)
Subjects: LCSH: Oddities--Juvenile literature. | Fantastic architecture--Juvenile literature. | Buildings, structures, etc.--Juvenile literature. | Framed structures--Juvenile literature. | Building design--Juvenile literature. | Curiosities and wonders--Juvenile literature.
Classification: DDC 720--dc23

CONTENTS

CHAPTER ONE

A FISHY MUSEUM

Architect Frank Gehry likes watching fish. He enjoys their curving, flowing motion through the water. He likes the way fish give the sense of motion even when they are not moving. Gehry likes fish so much that he has used them as inspiration for his building designs, which use curves instead of straight lines.

His best-known fish-inspired building is the Guggenheim Museum Bilbao in Bilbao, Spain. With more than 250,000 square feet (23,000 sq m) of floor space, this building has curved pillars and

The Guggenheim Museum Bilbao is built along the Nervión River, which flows into the Atlantic Ocean.

Besides museums such as the Guggenheim Museum Bilbao, Frank Gehry designed concert halls, office buildings, and houses.

rounded lines. The building is covered in shiny panels that shimmer like giant fish scales.

Gehry saw the building just before its opening in 1998. He wasn't sure if he liked the unusual building and wondered what he had done. He said it took him a few years to like the museum he had designed.

Still, when the museum opened, it was a huge success. The building was so popular that it boosted Bilbao's economy. Architecture experts have voted the Guggenheim Museum Bilbao as one of the greatest buildings of its time.

WHAT IS ARCHITECTURE?

People have built countless structures all over the world. Many are considered unremarkable. Everyday buildings can seem boring and predictable. Others are famous, known for their beauty or historical significance. And a few, such as the Guggenheim Museum Bilbao, have a reputation for looking weird.

Architects are the people who create buildings. They practice architecture, which is the art and science of designing and building structures, especially those used by people. Architects consider many things when designing a building.

POSTMODERN ARCHITECTURE

The Guggenheim Museum Bilbao is an example of a postmodern building. Postmodern architecture is a style of building design. It emerged in the 1970s and 1980s. Architects wanted to do something different from what had been done in the past. Postmodern buildings often combine other architectural styles in new and surprising ways. These buildings are often fun and whimsical.

FROM HATED TO LOVED

The world is home to several Guggenheim Museums. They are named after the Guggenheim family that funded these museums. The Solomon R. Guggenheim Museum in New York had a much rockier start than the Guggenheim Museum in Spain. It was built in 1959 and its design led to much controversy. It was compared to an inverted cupcake, a washtub without handles, and a giant Jell-O mold. One writer said the museum ruined the mood of the neighborhood. Today, the building is one of the most famous in the city. It was designated a New York City Landmark in 1990. It was placed on the World Heritage List in 2019.

One is the function of the building or structure. The function of a school is different from the function of a sports arena. The way these buildings tend to be designed is different too.

Architects also consider how a building can communicate ideas and feelings. For example, some buildings are designed to impress people. These structures can be very big or ornate. Buildings such as churches and community centers are often designed to make people feel welcome. Other buildings are meant to be fun, attract attention, or make people think. Architects express ideas and feelings through the style, size, and shape of the building, as well as the color and materials used inside and out. The result can be a structure that is both functional and artistic.

ADVENTUROUS ARCHITECTURE

Some architects try to build things unlike anything built before. The results of their work can seem odd. Some structures such as the Guggenheim Museum Bilbao have unusual curving shapes. Others may look like they are dancing, leaning, or melting. Some look like they've been cut in half. A few are built completely upside down.

Many weird buildings are in the shape of giant animals, foods, or household objects. There are buildings that look like a koala, dinosaur, teapot, or pair of high-heeled shoes. There's even a building

Mr. Toilet House's official name is *Haewoojae*, which means "a place of sanctuary where one can solve one's worries" in Korean.

shaped like a toilet in South Korea. Mr. Toilet House is a museum dedicated to, of course, toilets.

Some buildings are copies of famous landmarks. These include buildings that look like an Egyptian pyramid or a sphinx. Copies of the Eiffel Tower, Statue of Liberty, Leaning Tower of Pisa, and more dot cities across the world.

Not everyone likes weird buildings. Some people think they are eyesores. But many other people find weird buildings to be interesting and fun. Weird and unexpected buildings, houses, bridges, and other structures surprise and delight people around the world.

STRAIGHT TO THE
SOURCE

People do not always agree on what counts as postmodern architecture. Architect Michael Graves, who has been called a postmodern architect, said the following in a 2012 interview:

> *As an architect, when they say: "Are you a postmodernist" I always ask, "What is that?" And they don't know, they have no idea; it's just a name to them. . . . For me, postmodernism is a way to see the traditional city. . . . I think it's important that when we walk in the city, that we are part of the city, that the buildings of the city speak back to us. This is what I am after in my architecture.*

Source: Luke Arehart. "Thirty Years Later: A Conversation with Michael Graves About the Portland Building." *Portland Architecture*, 4 Dec. 2012, chatterbox.typepad.com. Accessed 30 Apr. 2025.

WHAT'S THE BIG IDEA?

Take a close look at this passage. What is Graves's point about what postmodern architecture means? What can you tell about the way he thinks about his own work? Why do you think people disagree about what qualifies as postmodern architecture?

www.krzywydomek.info
OSPES SALVE...
SO! COFFEE
Pyszne
naleśniki
wytrawne i słodkie
SO! COFFEE
SO SOCIAL
53
KRZYWY DOMEK
BLIKPOL

BIZARRE BUILDINGS

The Crooked House in Sopot, Poland, looks like it came straight from a fairy tale. In fact, the architects were inspired by the fairy-tale drawings of a Polish illustrator. The 43,000-square-foot (4,000 sq m) building looks as if it is melting and falling, but the building is very sound. Inside this whimsical building are shops, restaurants, and offices. The Crooked House is just one of many weird commercial buildings around the world.

The architects behind the Crooked House began designing it in 2001. By 2004, it was open to the public.

EPIC OFFICE BUILDINGS

The headquarters of software company Epic Systems near Verona, Wisconsin, looks a lot like an amusement park. Employees work in themed buildings across six campuses bearing names such as Storybook, Wizards Academy, and Farm. Buildings and decorations take their inspiration from films and books such as *Charlie and the Chocolate Factory*, *Harry Potter*, *The Hobbit*, and *Alice in Wonderland*. Visitors can take self-guided tours of the campuses and ride bikes painted to look like black-and-white cows.

A building in Orlando, Florida, looks like it was dropped upside down on the side of a street. It was built by the WonderWorks educational entertainment company. The company's slogan, "Let your imagination run wild," could be a motto for the building. Its design follows a story. Professor Wonder released a tornado inside his laboratory on a remote island in the Bermuda Triangle, a region associated with mysterious ship and plane disappearances. The strong winds carried it to

Besides the location in Orlando, the WonderWorks company has locations in places across the United States, including in Tennessee, South Carolina, New York, and Missouri.

Florida, where it eventually landed upside down near a street.

The WonderWorks building is an amusement park that contains more than 100 educational and entertaining exhibits. Visitors can land a National Aeronautics and Space Administration (NASA) shuttle in a simulation, rest on a surprisingly supportive

WORLD'S BIGGEST TENT

The world's biggest tent holds a huge shopping and entertainment center. The Khan Shatyr in Astana, Kazakhstan, is 492 feet (150 m) tall and looks like it is leaning. Inside the massive tent is 606,729 square feet (56,367 sq m) of space. The tent is filled with sunlight from the transparent walls, allowing many plants to grow inside. On average, more than 25,000 people visit Khan Shatyr every day. Visitors can shop, eat, and see a movie. They can also ride a roller coaster and sunbathe on a sandy beach inside the giant tent.

bed of 3,500 nails, and experience hurricane-force winds. They can also play laser tag, climb a ropes course, and eat dinner while watching a magic comedy show.

THE ATOMIUM

The Atomium in Brussels, Belgium's capital city, looks like an iron crystal that has been magnified 165 billion times. Each silver ball represents an iron atom. Tubes connect the atoms to create the cubic structure. The inside of the building resembles the interior of a spaceship or submarine. The 335-foot

The Atomium was designed by André Waterkeyn, André Polak, and Jean Polak.

(102 m) structure was built for the 1958 Brussels World's Fair. The fair's slogan was, "A world for a better life for mankind." The futuristic building was meant to represent a new world of peace and prosperity through science and technology.

The outside faces of Big Pants are crossed by steel braces that provide support.

The Atomium building declined over the years. It was renovated between 2004 and 2006. Today the building hosts three levels of exhibits. A viewing platform and restaurant provide panoramic views of Brussels. More than 800,000 people visit the building every year.

BIG PANTS

Skyscrapers are the tallest city buildings. A skyscraper in the middle of the business district of Beijing, China, is known as "Big Pants." The China Central Television headquarters building has two tall towers leaning toward each other. They are connected by a section across the top.

The building may have a funny nickname, but its construction was very serious. Connecting the three parts of the building was a great challenge. The building also had to be strong enough to withstand earthquakes. It took ten years to build.

FURTHER EVIDENCE

Chapter Two discusses the WonderWorks building. What was one of the main points of the chapter? Read the article at the link below. Does the information in the article support this point? Does it provide new evidence?

THE WONDERWORKS STORY

abdocorelibrary.com/weird-structures

ECCENTRIC HOUSES

Most houses and apartment buildings follow the same basic square design. But some houses are more creative. They turn the rule of house design on its head, sometimes literally. Weird houses are shaped like mushrooms, balls, toilets, and more. They rest in trees, sit on rocks in the water, and nestle in caves. House design is limited only by the imagination.

The Casa Batlló in Barcelona, Spain, looks like a work of art, but it is a fully functional home. The original structure was built in 1877.

Casa Batlló is one of the most visited sites in Barcelona, attracting one million visitors per year.

In 1903, Josep Batlló y Casanovas bought the house. He hired the architect Antoni Gaudí to renovate it. Gaudí changed the outside of the house. He made the balconies and pillars look like masks and bones. He covered the building in colorful bits of ceramic and glass. Inside the house are stained glass windows, curved walls, and skylights. Parts of the house have blue tiles and lighting that give the impression of standing underwater.

Casa Batlló is no longer used as a home. Visitors can tour the building and learn

DANCING HOUSE

The Dancing House in Prague, Czech Republic, looks like two people dancing. It may have been inspired by two famous dancers, Ginger Rogers and Fred Astaire. The glass tower held up by curved pillars represents Rogers, and the solid tower of rock is Astaire. The building also represents the country's transition from its Communist past. In 1945, a building on the site was bombed during World War II (1939–1945). The Dancing House replaced it in 1996. Not everyone approved. Some people felt the strange, wavy building was out of place among the other historic buildings.

Weird houses, such as the Dancing House, can be found all around the world.

about its history and architecture. Casa Batlló became a United Nations Educational, Scientific and Cultural Organization (UNESCO) World Heritage site in 2005.

The grounds surrounding Quetzalcoatl's Nest are full of lush plant life and landscaping features.

QUETZALCOATL'S NEST

Visitors to Mexico City can stay a few nights in a snake. The winding, iridescent building is called Quetzalcoatl's Nest. Its architect, Javier Senosiain, was inspired by the Aztec serpent god Quetzalcoatl. The house has bedrooms, bathrooms, a kitchen, and a living room spread across the head, belly, and tail of the serpent. Tunnels connect the rooms. The building winds around more than 165,000 square feet (15,300 sq m) of area. The grounds around the snake include gardens, lakes, and caves.

Quetzalcoatl's Nest is an example of Senosiain's bioarchitecture. This style of architecture emphasizes curving, natural forms in harmony with the surrounding landscape. His other creations include a home that looks like a spiral shell.

WINCHESTER MYSTERY HOUSE

Sarah Winchester was the widow of William Winchester, whose family owned the Winchester Repeating Arms Company, a firearm manufacturer. She bought a small two-story farmhouse near San Jose, California, in 1886. She began remodeling it, adding many new features over time. Almost 40 years later, it was a giant of a house with 160 rooms. The house has hidden rooms, secret passageways, and rumored sightings of ghosts of people killed by Winchester rifles.

One Cube House is open to visits by the public for a fee.

THE CUBE HOUSES

Unlike bioarchitecture's curving forms, the Cube Houses in Rotterdam, the Netherlands, boast geometry's hard angles. They were built after Dutch architect Piet Blom decided to design large apartments that would occupy the least amount of urban space possible. The result was a structure featuring many cubes tilted at more than 45 degrees.

The bright yellow apartments are perched on their bases above a major road through the city. The homes look like they could be cramped and unlivable, but they are spacious and airy with lots of natural light. Each of the 39 apartments has three bedrooms and living space spread over three levels connected by steep staircases.

EXPLORE ONLINE

Chapter Three focuses on a number of unusual homes and apartments, including the Casa Batlló in Spain. The website below explores the inside and outside of the house. It goes into more depth about its architect, design, and history. How is the information from the website the same as the information in Chapter Three? What new information did you learn from the website?

HISTORY OF CASA BATLLÓ

abdocorelibrary.com/weird-structures

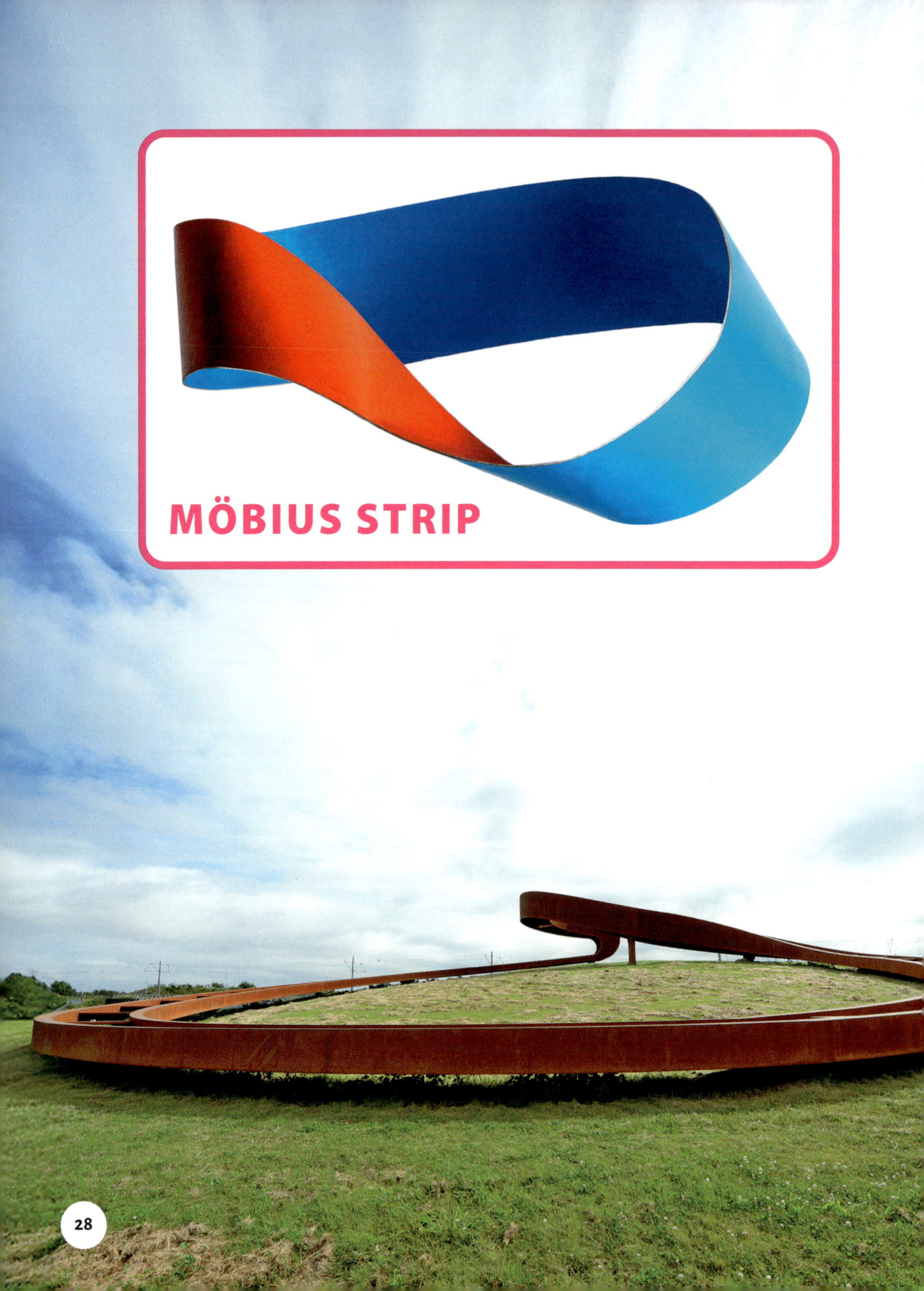
MÖBIUS STRIP

CHAPTER FOUR

UNUSUAL BRIDGES

Bridges help people safely cross water, railroad tracks, roads, and valleys. They connect communities. Bridges are designed to be strong and withstand all kinds of weather. Some are also designed to make crossing them an inspiring and fun experience.

The Elastic Perspective bridge sits on a hillside above the city of Rotterdam in the Netherlands. It was inspired by the Möbius strip. The Möbius strip is a loop formed by twisting a rectangular surface and connecting the ends. The result is a closed

The Möbius strip is named after the German mathematician who was one of the first to describe the figure's mathematical properties.

FREMONT TROLL

A giant troll lurks under the Aurora Bridge in Seattle, Washington. The Fremont Troll is 18 feet (5.5 m) tall and grasps a Volkswagen Beetle car. In the 1970s, Steve Badanes and his students designed and built the statue as part of a contest to help improve the neighborhood. The statue started a neighborhood tradition of celebrating Trolloween, a variant of Halloween.

loop with one surface and edge. The simple but surprising Möbius strip has inspired both mathematicians and artists, including the architect of the Elastic Perspective bridge. Walking up and down the staircase and along this bridge can feel like an endless trip to nowhere.

More an art project than a bridge, the rusty steel contraption folds around so that it appears to be one continuous loop. Looking at it from ground level, one has trouble telling the top from the bottom or the beginning from the end. For the architects who designed the bridge, this aspect represents a nearby suburb's relationship with the city of Rotterdam.

TYPES OF BRIDGES

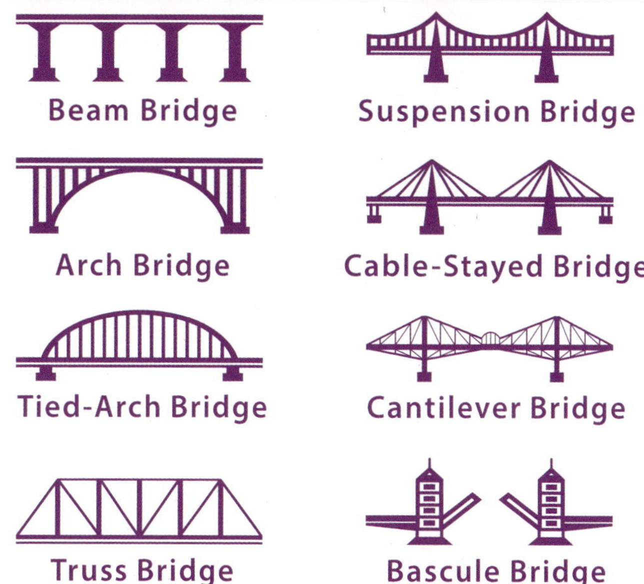

No matter how strange a bridge might look, it is designed to support heavy loads. This infographic shows different types of bridge designs. How are they similar and how are they different? How do you think the designs make them strong?

TIANJIN EYE

The Yongle Bridge in Tianjin, China, is more than a wide bridge across the Hai River. It's also an amusement park ride. The Tianjin Eye is a huge Ferris wheel. It is built above the six-lane Yongle Bridge.

The Tianjin Eye is one of the tallest Ferris wheels in the world. It is about 400 feet (120 m) tall. It is also

During each spectacle, the Dragon Bridge breathes fire nine times and spurts water three times.

the world's largest Ferris wheel on a bridge. The Eye has 48 cabins that rotate around the wheel. Each cabin can carry eight passengers. It takes 30 minutes for the Ferris wheel to make a single rotation. Drivers stuck in traffic on the bridge can enjoy watching people ride the Tianjin Eye.

DRAGON BRIDGE

A bridge in Da Nang, Vietnam, transforms into a fire-breathing dragon every weekend. The six-lane bridge across the Han River is shaped like a dragon. The dragon undulates along the entire length of the bridge that links the east and west sides of the city.

More than 15,000 lights make the Dragon Bridge glow every night. Every weekend and on major holidays, the Dragon Bridge breathes fire and spurts water. Fireworks burst above the Dragon Bridge during the annual Da Nang International Fireworks Festival.

LEGO BRIDGE

A bridge in Wuppertal, Germany, looks as if it were built from giant colorful LEGO bricks. Beneath this fun design is a common concrete bridge that was originally not very visually interesting. The city hired artist Martin Heuwold to paint it. He was inspired by his two daughters' LEGO bricks. The artist first got permission from the LEGO company. Then a team of painters spent two weeks transforming the 2,700-square-foot (250 sq m) structure into an eye-catching bridge of LEGO bricks. The formerly boring bridge is now a local landmark.

CHAPTER FIVE

DUCK ARCHITECTURE

In 1931, a farmer on Long Island, New York, constructed a building in the shape of a big white duck, where he could sell his ducks and eggs. This building was called the Big Duck. A new building style known as duck architecture, also called mimetic architecture, was born. The designs of these buildings advertise what is offered inside. Some examples of duck architecture include a hot dog stand that looks like a giant hot dog, a toad museum in the shape of a giant toad, and a donut-shaped bakery with a hole that cars can

In 1997, the Big Duck building was listed on the National Register of Historic Places. The US government maintains this list of notable places across the country.

drive through. Mimetic buildings are often near busy roads where they attract people driving by.

The Azerbaijan National Carpet Museum in Baku, Azerbaijan, looks like a giant rolled-up carpet. Inside is the world's largest collection of traditional carpets, all of which were made in the country. The eye-catching building took six years to build and opened in 2014.

The museum is dedicated to the art of carpet weaving. It stores, researches, and exhibits more

WORLD'S BIGGEST BASKET

One of the most famous examples of mimetic architecture is the Longaberger basket building in Newark, Ohio. It was built as the headquarters of the Longaberger Company, which made and sold baskets. The building is an exact replica of one of the company's baskets magnified 160 times. The Big Basket is seven stories high. Two steel handles top the basket and weigh 75 tons (68 metric tons). The Longaberger Company went out of business in 2018, but a developer bought the building and was considering how to use it in the 2020s.

The art of carpet weaving is considered a national symbol of Azerbaijan.

than 6,000 traditional rugs and carpets. It also contains exhibits on jewelry, embroidery, costume, and other national arts.

FISH BUILDING

A giant fish houses the headquarters for the National Fisheries Development Board in Hyderabad, India. The office building, known as the "fish building," was built in 2012. It looks like a big silver fish swimming through

The National Fisheries Development Board works to improve productivity in India's fish industry.

the air. The outside is covered in windows that resemble shimmering scales. The front of the building has an open mouth and blue glass eyes.

The fish building is several stories high. It is impressive by day and even more so by night. Blue spotlights shine on the building in the dark, making it look as if it's swimming through water across the city.

GIANT BOOKSHELF

Visitors to the Kansas City Public Library in Missouri can park in a giant bookshelf. The parking garage is painted to look like a row of huge books. The 22 book spines are 25 feet (7.6 m) tall and 9 feet (3 m) wide.

The garage was built in 2006, and the idea of a giant bookshelf came from public input. Community members voted on which book titles should appear on the building. The titles include classic works of literature by Charles Dickens, Mark Twain, Willa Cather, and others. Also featured are beloved children's books such as *Charlotte's Web, Little House on the Prairie, The Wonderful Wizard of Oz*, and *Green Eggs and Ham.*

THE BIG PINEAPPLE

South Africa hosts the world's largest pineapple. Bathurst, where the building is located, is known for growing pineapples. The Big Pineapple is made of metal and fiberglass and stands three stories tall. Inside is a museum dedicated to pineapples with pineapple products for sale. There is a similar huge pineapple building in Australia, but South Africa's is about two feet (0.6 m) taller.

From crooked and upside-down houses to dragon bridges to buildings shaped like food and animals, many fascinating and downright weird structures stand in the world. These structures showcase the imagination and creativity of architects everywhere. Weird buildings

WEIRD STRUCTURES AROUND THE WORLD

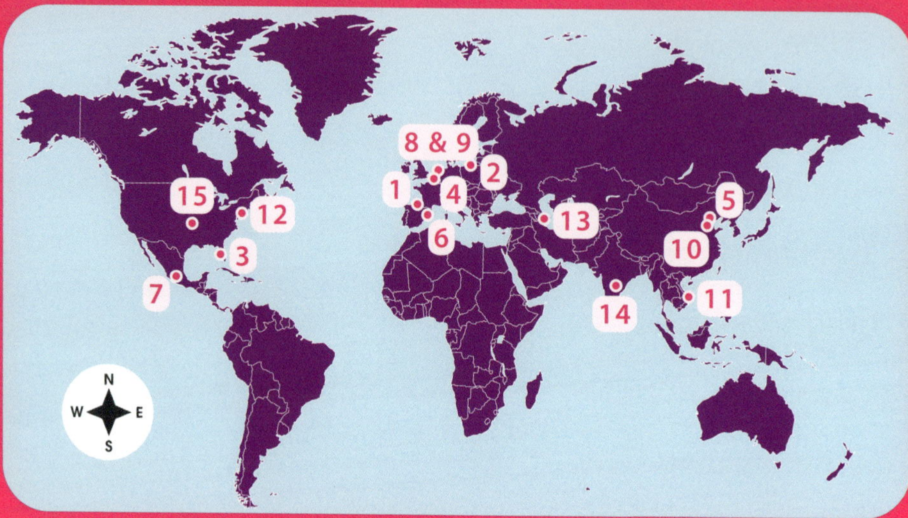

1. Guggenheim Museum Bilbao
2. Crooked House
3. WonderWorks building
4. Atomium
5. Big Pants
6. Casa Batlló
7. Quetzalcoatl's Nest
8. Cube Houses
9. Elastic Perspective bridge
10. Tianjin Eye
11. Dragon Bridge
12. Big Duck
13. Azerbaijan National Carpet Museum
14. National Fisheries Development Board
15. Kansas City Public Library

This map of the world shows where many weird structures are located. Are there any regions with no unusual structures noted? With some research, can you find more weird buildings to fill in the map?

challenge ideas about what's possible in building design, spark curiosity, and bring joy to people around the world.

STRAIGHT TO THE SOURCE

Aditya Rengaswamy got a chance to tour the office spaces packed into the Longaberger basket building in 2012. He found the tour and the quirky building very entertaining. He wrote:

> *This building represents all that is weird and fun in life. . . . Almost everyone was smiling and having fun. One of the employees even joked, "It's hard to take life too seriously when you work inside a basket!" I hate taking life too seriously, and I never want to forget the pure joy that each moment can provide. As a society, we should do more things that are purely silly and fun.*

Source: Aditya Rengaswamy. "The Breadbasket of Ohio." *Observer*, 19 Oct. 2012, observer.case.edu. Accessed 13 June 2025.

BACK IT UP

The author of this passage is using evidence to support a point. Write a paragraph describing the point the author is making. Then write down two or three pieces of evidence the author uses to make his point.

FAST FACTS

- Architects practice architecture, which is the art and science of designing and building structures.
- Structures are both functional and artistic, and creative buildings can brighten locations and make people think.
- Many weird buildings are examples of the postmodern style of architecture.
- The Atomium building is designed in the atomic structure of an iron crystal.
- Casa Batlló in Spain was renovated into a work of art by the famous architect Antoni Gaudí.
- All bridges must be safe and strong, even if they look like a dragon or are topped by a Ferris wheel.
- Duck architecture is also known as mimetic architecture, which is a building style designed to mimic what happens inside.
- Mimetic buildings often become roadside attractions visited by motorists and tourists.

STOP AND THINK

Tell the Tale

Chapter Three of this book discusses some interesting and surprising houses. Imagine that you live in one of these houses. Write 200 words about what it's like.

Surprise Me

This book discusses weird buildings and structures. After reading this book, what two or three facts about unusual architecture did you find most surprising? Write a few sentences about each fact. Why did you find them surprising?

Another View

This book talks about weird buildings, houses, bridges, and other structures. As you know, every source is different. Ask a librarian or another adult to help you find another source about unusual architecture. Write a short essay comparing and contrasting the new source's point of view with that of the book's author. How are they different and why?

Say What?

Studying unusual architecture can mean learning a lot of new vocabulary. Find five words in this book you've never heard before. Use a dictionary to find out what they mean. Then write the meaning in your own words and use each word in a new sentence.

GLOSSARY

atom
the basic unit of a chemical element

Communist
relating to Communism, a system of government in which a single ruling party controls the production of goods

controversy
something that causes a great deal of disagreement

iridescent
showing many bright colors that change based on how light hits the surface

landmark
a structure in a landscape that stands out

skyscraper
a very tall building

undulate
to move in a continuous, smooth up and down motion

whimsical
unusual, playful, and unpredictable

ONLINE RESOURCES

To learn more about weird structures, visit our free resource websites below.

Visit **abdocorelibrary.com** or scan this QR code for free Common Core resources for teachers and students, including vetted activities, multimedia, and booklinks, for deeper subject comprehension.

Visit **abdobooklinks.com** or scan this QR code for free additional online weblinks for further learning. These links are routinely monitored and updated to provide the most current information available.

LEARN MORE

Agrawal, Roma. *How Was That Built?: The Stories Behind Awesome Structures.* Bloomsbury Children's Books, 2022.

Allen, Peter. *Atlas of Amazing Architecture.* Cicada Books, 2021.

INDEX

About the Author

Yvette LaPierre lives in North Dakota and has written more than 30 books for young readers. She enjoys visiting her town's historic The Kegs Drive-In, which is shaped like two large wooden barrels.